DUDLEY SCHOOLS LIBRARY
AND INFORMATION SERVICE

KU-453-057

Schools Library and Information Services

S00000682960

DUDLEY SCHOOLS LIBRARY
AND INFORMATION SERVICE

A History of Super Science

Andrew Solway

Raintree

www.raintreepublishers.co.uk
Visit our website to find out more information about **Raintree** books.

To order:
☎ Phone 44 (0) 1865 888112
🖹 Send a fax to 44 (0) 1865 314091
💻 Visit the Raintree bookshop at **www.raintreepublishers.co.uk** to browse our catalogue and order online.

First published in Great Britain by Raintree, Halley Court, Jordan Hill, Oxford OX2 8EJ, part of Harcourt Education.
Raintree is a registered trademark of Harcourt Education Ltd.

© Harcourt Education Ltd 2006
The moral right of the proprietor has been asserted.

All rights reserved. No part of this publication may be reproduced, stored in a retrieval system, or transmitted in any form or by any means, electronic, mechanical, photocopying, recording, or otherwise, without either the prior written permission of the publishers or a licence permitting restricted copying in the United Kingdom issued by the Copyright Licensing Agency Ltd, 90 Tottenham Court Road, London W1T 4LP (www.cla.co.uk).

Editorial: Lucy Thunder and Richard Woodham
Design: Michelle Lisseter, Carolyn Gibson, and Bigtop
Illustrations: Seb Burnett
Picture Research: Melissa Allison and Fiona Orbell
Production: Camilla Crask

Originated by Dot Gradations Ltd
Printed and bound in Italy by Printer Trento srl

ISBN 1 844 43852 X
10 09 08 07 06
10 9 8 7 6 5 4 3 2 1

British Library Cataloguing in Publication Data
Solway, Andrew
A History of Super Science: scientific enquiry – materials
540
A full catalogue record for this book is available from the British Library.

Acknowledgements
The publishers would like to thank the following for permission to reproduce photographs:
Corbis pp. 4–5 (Royalty-Free), 13 (lower left) (Royalty-Free), 13 (lower right) (Royalty-Free), 13 (top left) (Royalty-Free), 19 (Archivo Iconografico, S.A.); Creatas p. 13 (top right); Science Photo Library pp. 6–7 (Dirk Wiersma), 16–17 (Sheila Terry), 20 (Andrew Lambert Photography), 23 (Sheila Terry), 26 (CCI Archives), 22–23 (US Department Of Energy), 24–25 (Sheila Terry); The Art Archive p. 14–15 (Metropolitan Museum of Art New York/Joseph Martin); The Bridgeman Art Library pp. 21 (The Royal Institution, London, UK), 10–11 (Derby Museum and Art Gallery, UK), 8–9 (Palazzo Vecchio (Palazzo della Signoria) Florence, Italy).

Cover photograph of a scientist, reproduced with permission of Comstock Images.

Illustrations by Seb Burnett.

The publishers would like to thank Nancy Harris and Harold Pratt for their assistance in the preparation of this book.

Every effort has been made to contact copyright holders of any material reproduced in this book. Any omissions will be rectified in subsequent printings if notice is given to the publishers.

The paper used to print this book comes from sustainable resources.

Disclaimer
All the Internet addresses (URLs) given in this book were valid at the time of going to press. However, due to the dynamic nature of the Internet, some addresses may have changed, or sites may have changed or ceased to exist since publication. While the author and publishers regret any inconvenience this may cause readers, no responsibility for any such changes can be accepted by either the author or the publishers.

- 48025

682960   SCH

JS40

Contents

Any words appearing in the text in bold, **like this**, are explained in the glossary. You can also look out for them in the word box at the bottom of each page.

Thick glasses and wild hair?

Cartoon scientists usually have thick glasses and wild hair. They are brilliant. But they don't know which way round their trousers go. Of course, real scientists are not like this. Or are they?

Chemists are scientists who are interested in **substances**. A substance is something that you can touch and see. Chemists look at how substances join together. They also look at how substances can be separated. Chemists have made some important discoveries in the past. They have also done some strange things.

Let's look at a few chemists. These chemists first found out about **atoms** and **elements**. But before we do, what are atoms and elements?

atom	tiny piece that makes up every kind of substance
element	substance made of only one kind of atom
substance	something that you can touch and see

5

Chemists use lots of glass test tubes and flasks. The washing up is a nightmare!

The simplest things

Everything around us is made of atoms. **Atoms** are the smallest parts of a **substance**. You could fit millions of atoms into the full stop at the end of this sentence. There are many different kinds of atoms.

An **element** is made of only one kind of atom. Elements are simple substances.

A few things in your house might be elements. The pans in your kitchen may be made of aluminium. Aluminium is an element. It is made of aluminium atoms and nothing else.

Most substances are not as simple as elements. They are made of more than one kind of atom.

Now that we know about atoms and elements, we can get back to those crazy chemists…

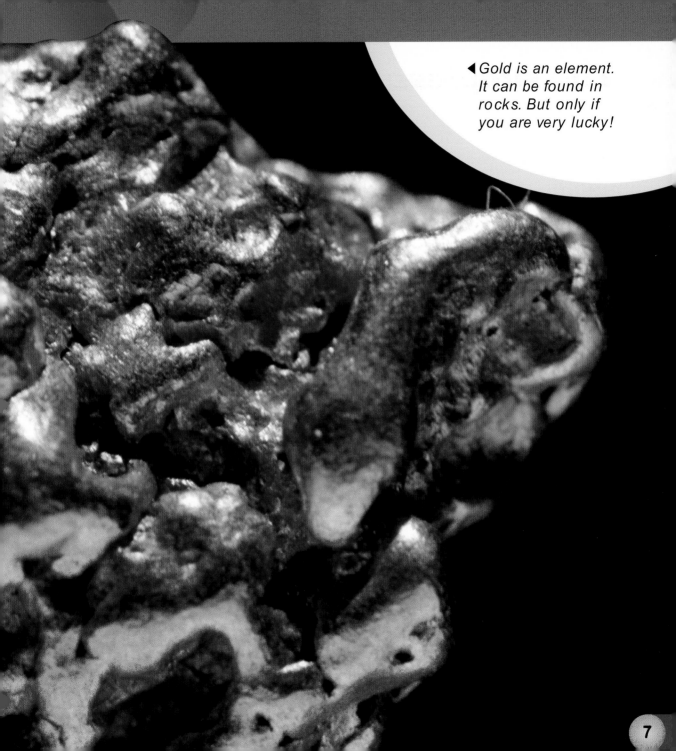

◄ *Gold is an element. It can be found in rocks. But only if you are very lucky!*

The first chemists

The earliest chemists were called **alchemists**. They did lots of mixing and heating of **substances**. A substance is something that you can touch and see. But alchemists were really interested in two things. They wanted to know how to live forever. They also wanted to know how to make gold!

Alchemists made some useful discoveries. Arnold of Villanova was an alchemist. He lived a long time ago. He had some pretty crazy ideas. He thought people could live for hundreds of years. To do so, a person had to rub themselves with spices. They also had to eat chickens that had been fed on snakes and vinegar!

Another alchemist was the first person we know of to discover an **element**…

◄ This is how an alchemist's workshop may have looked.

IOÁNES
STRATENSIS
FLANDRVS
1570

9

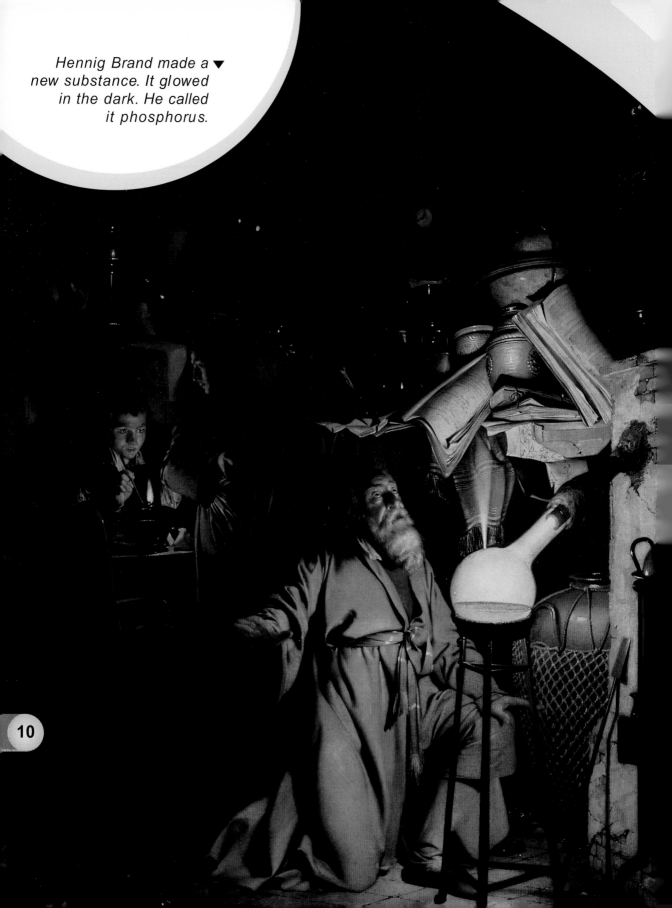

Hennig Brand made a ▼ new substance. It glowed in the dark. He called it phosphorus.

A golden liquid

Hennig Brand was a German **alchemist**. Like most alchemists, he wanted to make gold. He tried making gold from other metals. But this didn't work. So he decided to use another **substance**. He tried making gold from **urine**!

First he collected buckets of urine. He left them to sit for days. He then heated the urine. Next, Brand heated the urine at a high temperature. Some of the urine **evaporated**. It turned into a gas. Brand collected this gas and cooled it down. The gas became a solid when it cooled down.

The solid was white instead of gold. It also glowed in the dark! Brand had discovered a new **element**. He called it phosphorus.

▼ Brand collected many buckets of urine. He thought he could use urine to make gold.

11

evaporate   turn from a liquid into a gas
urine   mixture of water and unwanted chemicals from your body

Earth, fire, air, and water

Robert Boyle was an English **alchemist**. He lived about 400 years ago. He was rich, so he didn't try making gold. In one experiment he thought he had turned gold into another metal!

Boyle liked experimenting. He had a **laboratory** in his house. He did thousands of different experiments in it.

At that time, most people thought there were just four **elements**. They thought that earth (soil), fire, air, and water were the only elements. But Boyle wasn't so sure. His experiments made him think that this idea was wrong. Soon other chemists started to agree with him. But if air, fire, earth, and water were not elements, what were?

Tell-tale alchemist

Most alchemists kept their experiments secret. They never told anyone about them. But Boyle told everyone exactly how he did his experiments. He also told everyone what happened. Modern scientists now work in the same way.

laboratory   place for doing experiments

◀ *People used to think that fire, water, air, and earth were elements.*

13

On the boil

Antoine-Laurent Lavoisier was a French chemist. He was the first to sort out the **elements.** He lived about 100 years after Robert Boyle.

Lavoisier loved experiments. In one experiment he heated water until it **evaporated** and became a gas. He collected the gas and cooled it. The gas turned back into water again. He did this again and again for 101 days!

Lavoisier did this experiment many times for a reason. Some scientists believed that water could be heated and changed to soil. Lavoisier showed that this idea was wrong. He didn't make any soil. But you might think he was a bit crazy to spend 101 days boiling water!

This painting shows ▶ Lavoisier with his wife, Marie Anne. She helped with many of his experiments.

Real elements at last

Lavoisier found out lots of things from his own experiments. He also looked at experiments that other people had done. He used these experiments to work out new ideas.

Joseph Priestley was an English scientist. He showed that air was not a single **substance**. Lavoisier discovered that air was not an **element**. It could be split into many elements. Lavoisier also showed that water was not an element. He split water into two elements. These elements were hydrogen and oxygen.

Laviosier said that elements could not be split or broken down any further. He made a list of 33 substances that he thought were elements. Some of the elements in his list turned out to be wrong. But at last chemists were starting to understand elements.

17

◄ *Lavoisier is making water in this experiment. He is combining hydrogen and oxygen.*

What a gas!

Lavoisier thought there were 33 **elements**. But scientists soon found others. One of the first scientists to find new elements was Humphry Davy. He was an English chemist.

Davy first became known in 1799. He discovered a gas called nitrous oxide (laughing gas). He found that this gas could stop people feeling pain during operations.

Davy also discovered how to make powerful **batteries**. Early batteries were made from metal and chemicals. Davy used different metals and chemicals in his batteries. This made them more powerful.

Davy also showed how batteries made electricity. They made electricity because of **chemical reactions** inside them. A chemical reaction happens when chemicals join together or split apart. Chemical reactions make new **substances**. A substance is something that you can touch and see.

battery	something that makes electricity using chemicals and metals
chemical reaction	when chemicals join together or split apart to make new substances

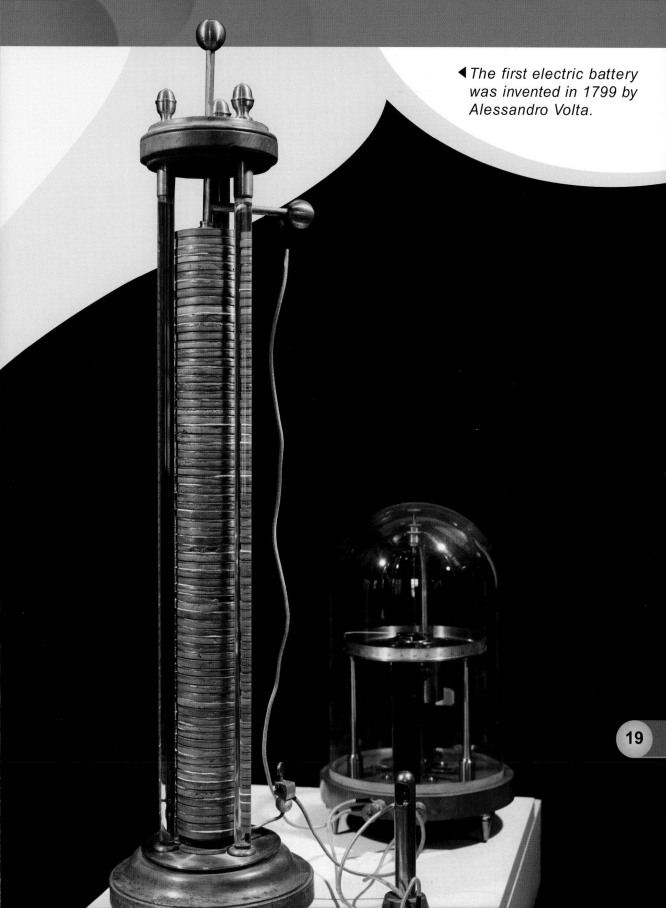

◀ *The first electric battery was invented in 1799 by Alessandro Volta.*

Electric elements

Davy tried to split **compounds**. Compounds are **substances** made from two or more **elements**. At first Davy put the compounds in water. Then he put electricity through the water. But the compounds did not split into elements.

Then Davy tried **melting** the compounds. He heated them until they became liquids. Success! The compounds split. He found two new elements called sodium and potassium. Later he found five more elements.

Davy discovered potassium. Potassium burns with a bright orange flame.

Up to 1,000 people ▲ would come to see Davy's talks.

Davy gave many talks about chemistry. People loved to watch Davy's experiments. The talks were very popular.

Chemists were at last beginning to understand elements. But they still didn't know very much about **atoms**.

Weighing atoms

John Dalton was an English chemist. His ideas about **atoms** were different. He found that the atoms of different **elements** were different sizes. He even weighed them! Well, sort of…

Dalton worked out what each element weighed compared to hydrogen. He knew that hydrogen was the lightest element. He knew it had the lightest atoms. Dalton did not know the actual weight of a hydrogen atom. He just set the weight as one.

Then he worked out the weights of other atoms compared to hydrogen. Carbon is an element. Carbon has an **atomic weight** of twelve. This means that an atom of carbon weighs twelve times more than an atom of hydrogen.

Billions of atoms

Today scientists know the actual weights of atoms. They are pretty light! There are 50,000,000,000,000,000,000,000 (50,000 billion billion) atoms in 1 gram of carbon.

atomic weight   weight of an atom compared to the weight of a hydrogen atom

◀ *Scientists can now see atoms using powerful microscopes. The different colours in this photo show different types of atoms.*

23

Dalton lived at about ▶ the same time as Humphry Davy.

The amazing chemist

Jons Berzelius was a teacher in Sweden. He lived at the same time as Humphry Davy and John Dalton. Berzelius discovered more **elements** than Davy. He also found that some of Dalton's **atomic weights** were wrong.

Berzelius also thought of a new way of writing the names of chemicals. He used symbols. The symbols used either one or two letters. They made writing the names of elements and **compounds** much easier.

Berzelius was ▶ really keen on teaching chemistry. He made sure it was taught in schools!

How symbols can help

Chemical symbols can show what is in a compound. Water is a compound. Water is made of two atoms of hydrogen (symbol H). These are joined to one atom of oxygen (symbol O). Water can be written in chemical symbols as H_2O.

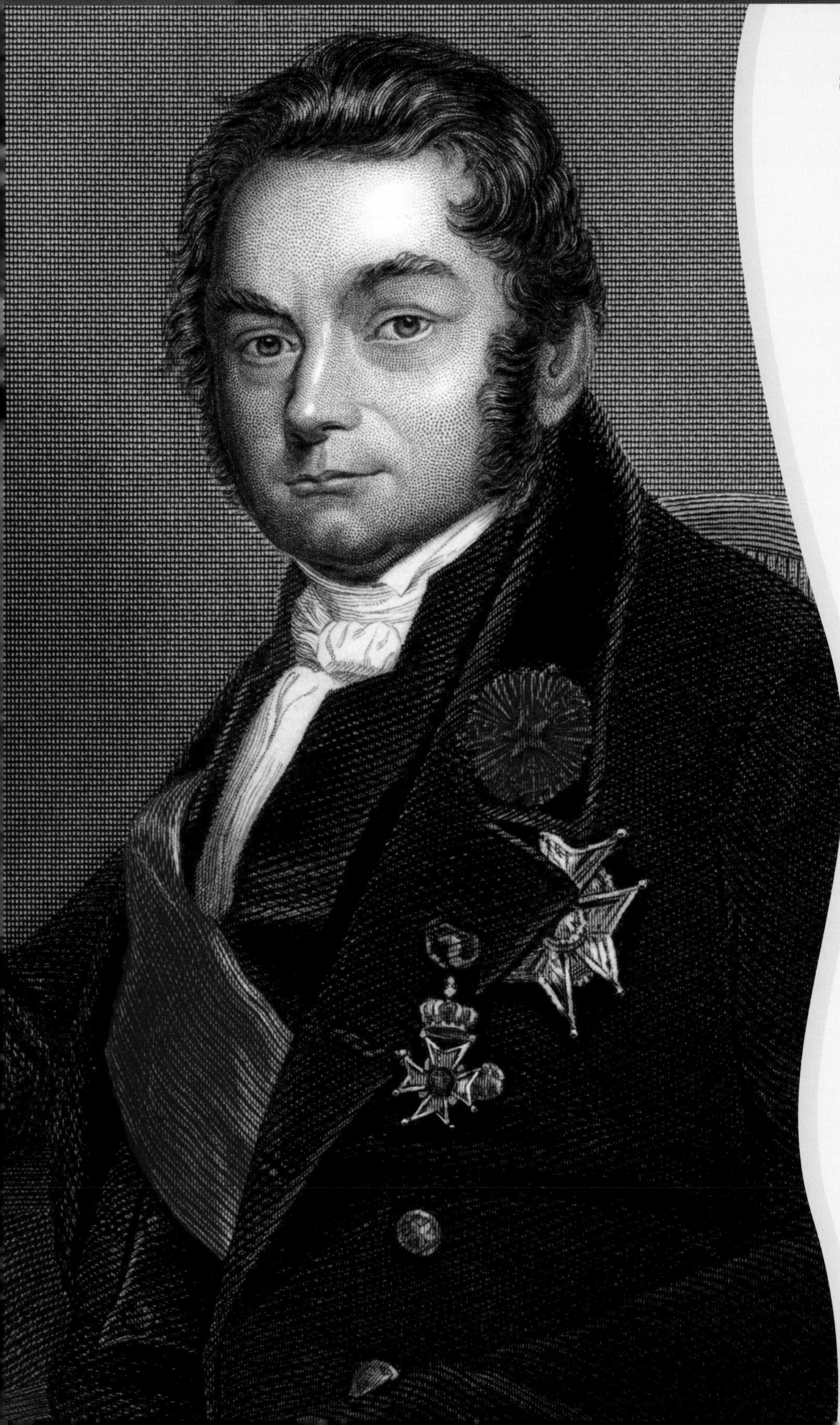

H

hydrogen

C

carbon

O

oxygen

Ca

calcium

Na

sodium

Fe

iron

Au

gold

Making sense of the elements

Dmitri Mendeleev was a Russian chemist. He came up with a way to group the **elements**.

Mendeleev grouped the elements in order of their **atomic weight**. He discovered that every seventh element was similar. For example, element 2 (lithium) was similar to element 9 (sodium). Element 3 (beryllium) was like element 10 (magnesium). So he organized the elements into a table of seven columns. He called it the **Periodic Table**.

Mendeleev was ▶ probably the hairiest chemist ever! At one time Russians were asked to shave off their beards. Mendeleev refused!

The Periodic Table helped chemists to understand the elements. Below is is part of Mendeleev's original Periodic Table. The numbers are the atomic weights. Compare it with the modern Periodic Table on page 28.

Period	Group 1	Group 2	Group 3	Group 4	Group 5	Group 6	Group 7
1	H hydrogen 1						
2	Li lithium 7	Be beryllium 9.4	B boron 11	C carbon 12	N nitrogen 14	O oxygen 16	F fluorine 19
3	Na sodium 23	Mg magnesium 24	Al aluminium 27.3	Si silicon 28	P phosphorus 31	S sulphur 32	Cl chlorine 35.5
4	K potassium 39	Ca calcium 40	– [unknown] 44	Ti titanium 48	V vanadium 51	Cr chromium 52	Mn manganese 55
5	(Cu) copper 63	Zn zinc 65	– [unknown] 68	– [unknown] 72	As arsenic 75	Se selenium 78	Br bromine 80

Periodic Table way of grouping the elements

The Periodic Table

The modern **Periodic Table** is a bit different from Mendeleev's. Many more elements have been discovered since Mendeleev created his table.

1 1.01 **H** Hydrogen								
3 6.94 **Li** Lithium	4 9.01 **Be** Beryllium							
11 22.99 **Na** Sodium	12 24.31 **Mg** Magnesium							
19 39.10 **K** Potassium	20 40.08 **Ca** Calcium	21 44.96 **Sc** Scandium	22 47.90 **Ti** Titanium	23 50.94 **V** Vanadium	24 51.996 **Cr** Chronium	25 54.94 **Mn** Manganese	26 55.85 **Fe** Iron	27 58.93 **Co** Cobalt
37 85.47 **Rb** Rubidium	38 87.62 **Sr** Strontium	39 88.91 **Y** Yttrium	40 91.22 **Zr** Zirconium	41 92.91 **Nb** Niobium	42 95.94 **Mo** Molybdenum	43 98 **Tc** Technetium	44 101.07 **Ru** Ruthenium	45 102.91 **Rh** Rhodium
55 132.91 **Cs** Caesium	56 137.33 **Ba** Barium	57 138.91 **La** Lanthanum	72 178.49 **Hf** Hafnium	73 180.95 **Ta** Tantalum	74 183.85 **W** Tungsten	75 186.21 **Re** Rhenium	76 190.20 **Os** Osmium	77 192.22 **Ir** Iridium
87 223 **Fr** Francium	88 226.03 **Ra** Radium	89 227.03 **Ac** Actinium	104 261 **Rf** Rutherfordium	105 262 **Db/Ha** Dubnium (Hahnium)	106 266 **Sg** Seaborgium	107 264 **Bh** Bohrium	108 269 **Hs** Hassium	109 268 **Mt** Meitnerium

58 140.12 **Ce** Cerium	59 140.91 **Pr** Praseodymium	60 144.24 **Nd** Neodynium	61 145 **Pm** Promethium	62 150.35 **Sm** Samarium	63 151.96 **Eu** Europium
90 232.04 **Th** Thorium	91 231.04 **Pa** Protactinium	92 238.03 **U** Uranium	93 237.05 **Np** Neptunium	94 244 **Pu** Plutonium	95 243 **Am** Americium

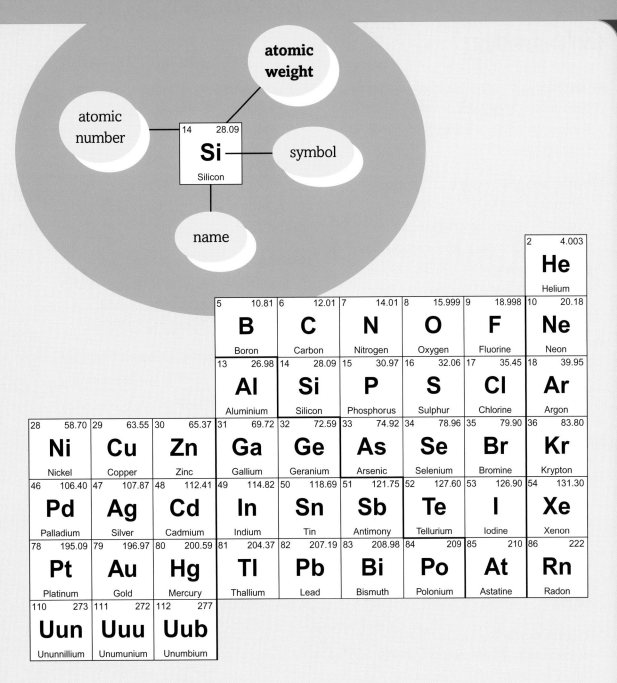

atomic number

atomic weight

14	28.09
Si	
Silicon	

symbol

name

2	4.003
He	
Helium	

5	10.81	6	12.01	7	14.01	8	15.999	9	18.998	10	20.18
B		**C**		**N**		**O**		**F**		**Ne**	
Boron		Carbon		Nitrogen		Oxygen		Fluorine		Neon	
13	26.98	14	28.09	15	30.97	16	32.06	17	35.45	18	39.95
Al		**Si**		**P**		**S**		**Cl**		**Ar**	
Aluminium		Silicon		Phosphorus		Sulphur		Chlorine		Argon	

28	58.70	29	63.55	30	65.37	31	69.72	32	72.59	33	74.92	34	78.96	35	79.90	36	83.80
Ni		**Cu**		**Zn**		**Ga**		**Ge**		**As**		**Se**		**Br**		**Kr**	
Nickel		Copper		Zinc		Gallium		Geranium		Arsenic		Selenium		Bromine		Krypton	
46	106.40	47	107.87	48	112.41	49	114.82	50	118.69	51	121.75	52	127.60	53	126.90	54	131.30
Pd		**Ag**		**Cd**		**In**		**Sn**		**Sb**		**Te**		**I**		**Xe**	
Palladium		Silver		Cadmium		Indium		Tin		Antimony		Tellurium		Iodine		Xenon	
78	195.09	79	196.97	80	200.59	81	204.37	82	207.19	83	208.98	84	209	85	210	86	222
Pt		**Au**		**Hg**		**Tl**		**Pb**		**Bi**		**Po**		**At**		**Rn**	
Platinum		Gold		Mercury		Thallium		Lead		Bismuth		Polonium		Astatine		Radon	
110	273	111	272	112	277												
Uun		**Uuu**		**Uub**													
Ununnillium		Unumunium		Unumbium													

64	157.25	65	158.93	66	162.50	67	164.93	68	167.26	69	168.93	70	173.04	71	174.97
Gd		**Tb**		**Dy**		**Ho**		**Er**		**Tm**		**Yb**		**Lu**	
Gadolinium		Terbium		Dysprosium		Holmium		Erbium		Thulium		Ytterbium		Lutetium	
96	247	97	247	98	251	99	252	100	257	101	258	102	259	103	262
Cm		**Bk**		**Cf**		**Es**		**Fm**		**Md**		**No**		**Lr**	
Curium		Berkelium		Californium		Einsteinium		Fermium		Mendelevium		Nobelium		Lawrencium	

Glossary

alchemist person who tried to make gold from other substances. Alchemists also tried to find out how to live forever.

atomic weight weight of an atom compared to the weight of a hydrogen atom. Hydrogen has an atomic weight of 1, and carbon has an atomic weight of 12. This means that carbon atoms are twelve times heavier than hydrogen atoms.

atom tiny piece that makes up every kind of substance. An atom is so small that you could fit millions of atoms into a full stop.

battery something that makes electricity using chemicals and metals. Batteries are used to power many everyday objects.

chemical reaction when chemicals join together or split apart to make new substances. A chemical reaction happens when iron rusts.

compound chemical that is made of two or more elements joined together. Water is a compound made of the two elements, hydrogen and oxygen.

element substance made of only one kind of atom. Metals such as copper and aluminium are common elements.

evaporate turn from a liquid into a gas. Heating often makes a liquid evaporate, like a puddle drying out in the sun.

laboratory place for doing experiments. Laboratories are usually specially built, and have scientific equipment for doing experiments.

melt turn from solid to liquid. Heating often makes a solid melt, like melting butter in a saucepan.

Periodic Table way of grouping the elements. The Periodic Table was created by Dmitri Mendeleev.

substance something that you can touch and see. Everything around you is made from substances.

urine mixture of water and unwanted chemicals from your body

Want to know more?

Books

- *Fizz, Bubble and Flash: Element Explorations and Atom Adventures for Hands-On Science Fun*, Anita J. Brandolini (Williamson, 2003).
- *Horrible Science: Chemical Chaos*, Nick Arnold (Scholastic Hippo, 1997)
- *Young Oxford Library of Science: Atoms and Elements*, David Bradley and Ian Crofton (Oxford, 2002)

Websites

- www.homepage.mac.com/dtrapp/Elements/elements.html
  Some of this website is hard to read. But if you want to know who discovered an element, this is the place to go.
- www.education.jlab.org/itselemental/
  Click on an element to find out all about it. There are also some element games.

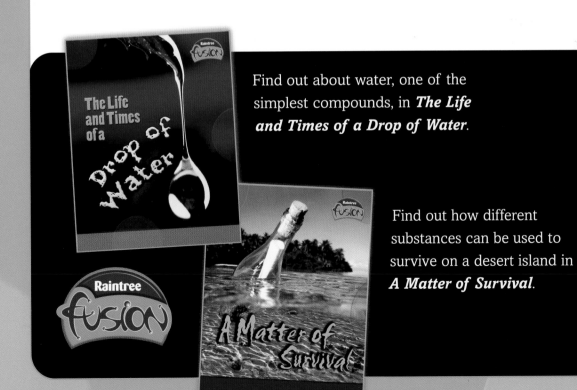

Find out about water, one of the simplest compounds, in *The Life and Times of a Drop of Water*.

Find out how different substances can be used to survive on a desert island in *A Matter of Survival*.

Index